UNSTRUCTURED
The Power of
Informal Learning

J. Nathan Rogers, PhD

A GOSHEN PUBLISHERS BOOK   VIRGINIA

Unstructured
The Power of Informal Learning

ISBN: 978-1-7370949-5-1
Copyright ©2021 J. Nathan Rogers, PhD

Library of Congress Cataloging-in-Publication Data

Published in 2021 by:

GOSHEN PUBLISHERS LLC
P.O. Box 1562
Stephens City, Virginia, USA
www.GoshenPublishers.com

Our books may be purchased in bulk for promotional, educational, or business use. For inquiries, please contact the publisher via email: Agents@GoshenPublishers.com.

First Edition 2021

Cover designed by Goshen Publishers LLC

Printed in the United States of America

UNSTRUCTURED
The Power of
Informal Learning

J. Nathan Rogers, PhD

Contents

FOREWORD

Dr. Rogers is a compelling writer who makes the informal learning journey a reality. With extensive experience in the field, it is no wonder that it was hard for me to put this book down.

Having known Dr. Rogers for years, I was not surprised by how informative this book is. Dr. Rogers's personal story on the informal learning journey and the struggle he experienced in school resonates with me. I was that student who wished my teachers had the training and resources he recommends.

As an educator in the K-12 field, I find this book extremely resourceful and empowering. For many in my field, we are conditioned to believe that learning is only effective through formal education. This book reveals many areas of informal learning that are overlooked but powerful if utilized.

For those in the cooperate arena, you are going to find this book resourceful as well. The power of informal learning as Dr. Rogers prescribes will propel you and your team to excel in all areas.

Dr. Christine Cloar

1. WHY INFORMAL LEARNING?

You are sitting in an advanced algebra class looking around the room, listening to the cheerful students' banter, wondering why you are feeling like a math fraud who should not be there. You are sure they will discover your lack of math knowledge.

Sitting in a kick-off meeting for a new project you are about to lead, you nod confidently as your boss summarizes the project objectives of a technology called Machine Learning (ML). He requests you provide the capability to process running live data points into a machine-learning algorithm to calculate an output such as a single numerical score. You feel completely lost and you do not know how you will learn this technology.

At some point in our academic or professional lives it has happened, and I am going to go out on a limb to say that it did not feel good. As you sat looking around the room, you asked yourself, am I the only one who does not understand this stuff? Of course, that did not stop your outward display of confidence, playing it off as if nothing was wrong and that you understood everything perfectly. If you are like most of us, you waited until you were home to go into a total meltdown, frantically trying to figure out how you are going to learn that topic or concept in time to be successful.

I am guessing you chose this book because you want a better way to learn and a better way to take control of your learning with confidence. Good news! You are not alone. When you master this framework, you will discover why you will never be alone again when it comes to learning and acquiring new knowledge and skills. René Descartes, a French-born philosopher, once said,"It is not enough to have a good mind, the main thing is to use it well." You have a good mind; I want to help you use it well. Self-directed learning is an alternative to structured methods. I will present a framework and strategy to guide you into a new way of thinking about learning, so you can be well on your way to confidence through self-driven learning.

The underlying assumption for this book is that many learners understand the challenges they face and are seeking a solution. This book further assumes that learners are unaware of a wide array of methods and technologies to continually acquire new skills and knowledge and meet their learning needs outside formal learning structures.

I wrote this book reflecting on my own learning journey with experiences spanning elementary, high school, college, and my professional career. I thought about the countless times I had no idea how to bridge what I was learning in an educational or workplace setting and the supporting knowledge I needed to be successful.

The knowledge gap is the missing piece of information that provides complete understanding of something. For example, you are unable to successfully solve an algebraic equation because you do not understand what it means to divide both sides of an equation by a specific variable. Understanding this concept and how to do this represents closing a knowledge gap.

I was not unintelligent, I was lacking the framework and tools needed to bridge that learning gap. It was these experiences and my desire to help others that led me to a doctorate in education. I focused my research on Informal Learning (IL). I am sharing these experiences as a practical and powerful application for your enrichment and likely economic success.

Who is the target audience of this book? First and foremost, individuals who desire to charter their course of learning for success and opportunities. It is directed to an audience of anyone interested in self-managed learning: parents, students, educators, corporate human resources and learning and development professionals, adult education and literacy providers, workforce development professionals, and entrepreneurs.

IL can be viewed as a strategy that co-exists with formal instructional programs for increased knowledge and skills attainment. It can also be a path for success in the absence of formal learning if used effectively. This book delves into how that works.

Reimagine the learning landscape for personal empowerment; people are successful in knowledge and skills acquisition when they take control of their learning journeys when, how, and for what reasons they believe it to be essential for success.

Now, let's start the conversation with an understanding of our learning model.

What comes to mind when you hear the term *informal*? The first thought probably lands around clothing, wearing something casual in nature. Minus the clothing part, you are in the target zone. IL has various meanings to different people. When I was a doctoral student conducting research using instructional designers as study participants, I posed the question "what is your understanding of *informal learning?*"

As expected, responses varied widely in response to the question. (Appendix A: Participants' Understanding of Informal Learning) But a unifying theme was the idea that this form of independent learning is initiated and controlled by the individual. It is outside of the formal learning structures that involve classrooms, teachers, or institutions and is defined by its very unstructured nature.

The importance of this type of knowledge building is a combination of learning relationships, learning networks and communities, self-directed learning, methods of learning, and technology integration. What should be clear to you is the unstructured nature described by the participants will be different for everyone. This may seem to be a chaotic way to learn anything. Rest assured, there is a way to bring a framework to IL without giving up its unstructured nature. The mix of self-guided opportunities and methods can form the foundational basis of self-fulfillment for academic and career success.

Let us take a journey of the familiar formal educational system we've all experienced. It has been the path for success for millions of people and will continue to be for many more years to come. Formal education enables us to gain the basic knowledge, skills, and social foundations of society. It is a key to success if we are willing to go the distance to learn all we can and put that learning to good use.

Unfortunately, all formal education is not equal, and I quickly discovered that not all parents are equally equipped to assist their children in the subjects required in their academic curriculums.

I recall my own experience in middle school with Mr. Johnson (not his real name). Mr. Johnson spent little time teaching; he filled most of the math class hour with jokes. It brought a lot of fun and laughter to the classroom, but it did little to advance my understanding of algebra and consequently I struggled with my homework. My parents were not able to assist me with math assignments. It was a painful undertaking and I suffered for years trying to make up the lost learning time.

I struggled through Blinn College, a small junior college in Texas, leaving with a 2.0 grade point average and an associate degree in business. After college I entered the United States Air Force. I found this was a great time for self-reflection, not only about where my future was going, but my plans to continue my education. I needed a new attitude and more. What I quickly learned in the Air Force is that one takes on responsibilities earlier than in the civilian world and it required me to grow up fast.

All was not lost in the college courses I took and one of the best classes I had was computing. Little did I know, it would come in handy in the Air Force. Back in the early 1980s, personal computers were on the scene in the Air Force and the security police and law enforcement field was the last bastion of resistance of technology at Kirtland Air Force Base. While the computer course I had in school was on an IMB 3742 with punch cards, it gave me the framework to think about how computers worked.

This certainly did not make me a personal computer genius, but senior officers had even less experience working with computers than I did. My unit commander had the foresight and instinct to realize that if any age group was likely to have experience with computers it would be within the younger age groups in the lower ranks. I applied for the position, was hired, and my new horror began. As excited as I was, I was an E-2, Airman First Class. An Airman First Class with an associate degree who was now expected to set hundreds of computers on desks across the organization, install software, and develop and teach everyone how to use a personal computer. Suddenly the excitement and feeling of prestige in being selected by a full bird colonel and assigned to his right hand, a lieutenant colonel, left me feeling once again inadequate and looking for a stage-left exit before the fraud I felt inside was exposed.

I remember about thirty days into the role calling my Aunt Mamie after work one day in a full-blown panic attack saying, "Oh God, I have bitten off more than I can chew with this computing job." Being the rock that Aunt Mamie always has been to me, she calmly said, "It will be all right. You are smart and you can do this. All you need to do is stop looking at the big picture and break this into smaller pieces and learn a little at a time while you implement what you are doing."

Thank God for Aunt Mamie. Her words not only wrapped around me like a comforting blanket, but they also felt like a life saver. Her words provided a boost to my desperately needed self-confidence. At that moment, I decided I have the power to control my learning; I started doing something that I did not have a name for, yet.

Partnering with a programmer at the base's computing center, Jim taught me all about computers, guided me to resources, and allowed me to explore and fill the learning gaps. I used his expertise and applied experiential learning. He was part of my self-learning network.

Coincidentally, this was the time in my life when I was bitten by the training bug that eventually became the cornerstone of my successful instructional design career. Instructional designers are responsible for creating courses and developing all the instructional materials, including participant guides, handouts, job aids, and developing all resources needed to facilitate the learning process. I served in the computing role as the computer systems manager for four years and during that time the innovation, implementation, and training I delivered to the security police group brought me recognition and praise to the level of 23rd Air Force. Twice in two years I was honored with the Air Force Achievement Medal. I had used IL without even knowing it!

I found my lost confidence with this new learning tool and I used it going forward together with my academic career.

I went on to study accounting; I was no longer haunted by math or any other learning endeavor. I graduated with a bachelor's degree in business with a major in accounting with a 3.37 grade point average (G.P.A.), an M.B.A in technology management with a 3.4, a Master of Education, 3.8, and finally my doctorate with a 3.78 G.P.A. There was no stopping me! What I have learned is it takes only one positive spark to change the direction of your life. Unbeknownst to me, that thing I could not name, Informal Learning, had a profound impact on my life.

It is ironic that by the time I was a doctoral student one of my favorite classes was statistics since it used equations from algebra. This was the last class of my doctoral program before advancing to the research phase. I was excited and relieved knowing I would pass the class with ease, and I did, with an A-. Although that was a happy ending considering my time with Mr. Johnson, it does not take away the memory of the pain, struggles, and feelings of inadequacy.

Learning requires meeting people where they are and ensuring they have the resources and proper framework for success. Adults generally seek out knowledge based on their personal needs; youth in most cases require more prompting and guidance, particularly when it comes to schoolwork. The one common denominator for both adults and youth are the skills required for the twenty-first century, so let us begin.

2. INFORMAL LEARNING AND THE ROLE OF TWENTY-FIRST CENTURY SKILLS

The complexity of today's work environment, and the functioning of society in general, requires us to solve problems under greater professional pressure than ever before in an increasingly technological world. In today's workforce, more than $1.2 trillion dollars is generated by people participating in what is called a gig or free-lance economy, defined as an economy based on independent contract labor.

The freelance or gig economy trend is a testament to the success of many who are not formally educated with college degrees, and *Informal Learning* (IL) is essential to sustaining their employability and success with technology.

Thinking about twenty-first century skills graphically, we might visualize them in two categories, interpersonal and literacy, where both categories require our ability to control them in the personal learning environments we build.

FIGURE 1 — 21st Century Skills

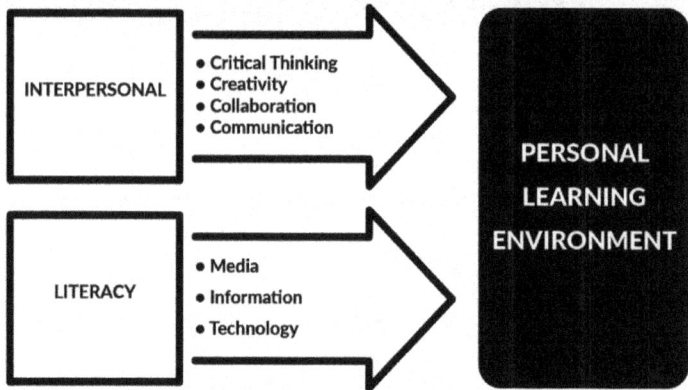

| INTERPERSONAL | • Critical Thinking
• Creativity
• Collaboration
• Communication | | PERSONAL LEARNING ENVIRONMENT |
| LITERACY | • Media
• Information
• Technology | | |

Non-formal education and training is an increasingly important component in corporate settings and is a vital part of the way adults continue to acquire new skills and knowledge. An example of this is seen with the constant technology change in organizations. There may not be formal training associated with every aspect of a specific technology implementation and it may require you to be self-driven to understand and use it.

Unfortunately, non-formal learning has not become an equal partner in human resources learning and development strategies. Employers know what they need you to learn to successfully fulfill their mission, but often that learning path does not plug all the gaps you need. For example, your employer may require you to attend machine learning training. Sending you to such a class without giving you an opportunity to close the knowledge gap that forms the foundations diminishes your likelihood of success. With more frequency, employees make the choice to engage in learning activities that are not imposed by their employers or formal educators. Whether you are seeking a new framework for learning within an organization, K-12 or college, on your own for enrichment, or for the entrepreneurial landscape, it requires the right skills.

These skills also are highly relevant to a successful self-guided process which will become apparent later in our discussion of building personal learning environments. If you Google "twenty-first century skills," many examples are given. I think that of all the inclusive skills to consider, the core set should include:

- Critical Thinking
- Creativity
- Collaboration
- Communication
- Information Literacy
- Media Literacy
- Technology Literacy

Interpersonal: Critical Thinking

One of the most thought-provoking definitions I have encountered on critical thinking is articulated by Richard Paul and Linda Elder stating, "Critical thinking is the art of thinking about thinking while thinking to make thinking better." Sit back for a moment and mentally marinate on this definition. What a powerful concept that integrates the process of analyzing, evaluating, and improving thinking.

Critical thinking allows us to analyze information and data to make decisions with strategic purposeful intention. For both students and employees, it forces us to evaluate our thought process which is crucial to our learning strategies. I believe possessing strong critical thinking skills are complementary to promoting creative thinking. The ongoing debate of whether creativity is inherited or acquired is not likely to be settled anytime soon.

Interpersonal: Creativity

Psychology Today characterized creativity in a way that best resonates with me.

> "An act of creativity can be grand and inspiring, such as creating a beautiful painting or designing an innovative new product. But an idea need not be artistic or world-changing to count as creative."[1]

The most important phrase of this definition is "an idea need not be artistic or world-changing to count as creative.[1]" From the context of self-learning, creativity will enable you to visualize various options of learning and how it effectively fits within the learning structures you create.

For example, I am thinking about putting together a small group of like-minded learners. The group explores a topic and uses learning and sharing tools like Zoom for discussions with participant visuals, voice, and screen sharing capabilities. There is no limitation to the imaginative ways your creativity can be used to structure your learning activities with a variety of resources. Creativity is manifested in the collaborative group example; seeking a way to share knowledge to collaborate to learn a topic.

So in the context of self-learning, what do we mean by collaboration and what is its purpose?

Interpersonal: Collaboration

Collaboration is a key component of self-efficacy, or believing in oneself, representing a measure of an individual's confidence in their ability to be successful with complex tasks. In our daily work or school life roles, we consistently are faced with ambiguous and complex problems, particularly with new technology, and those challenges can potentially impact our success and capability. Personal Learning Environments (PLEs) serve as valuable approaches to enhancing your effectiveness and building success in professional and academic roles through collaboration.

PLEs are an integral component of creating a social environment used to foster collaboration, providing opportunities for acting upon what is learned, promoting reflection, and integrating new knowledge into the personally-constructed learning environment. By strengthening collaboration, you have an opportunity for the inclusion of self-sourced study lessons, resources and experiential sessions, and demonstration labs to enhance your PLEs.

In today's world, learning is not limited solely to individual-to-individual and the exchange of knowledge; rather, it is reinforced by technologies that advances social interactions. These interactions are inextricably linked to both formal and non-formal instruction.

It is important to understand the components of social learning. Observation means discerning what is to be learned). Retention means internalizing information in our memories. Reproduction refers to the ability to actuate what was learned. Motivation is response to incentive for learning. Collectively, these components promote self-efficacy.

Interpersonal: Communication

As you are likely noticing at this point, all of the key points of twenty-first century skills are interconnected. We have linked critical thinking to creativity, and creativity to collaboration. And what is more important to these elements than communication skills?

We talk to people every day, and there always are ample opportunities for miscommunication. If you are engaging in a PLE, it is important to effectively communicate if real and meaningful learning is to occur in a group situation.

Dr. Davison Munodawafa of the World Health Organization says, "Communication involves transmission of verbal and non-verbal messages.

It consists of a sender, a receiver and channel of communication . . . provide opportunities for interpersonal interaction are likely to yield desired behavior change . . . communications include drama, song, storytelling, and debate, among others. The interpersonal communication can take into consideration social, cultural, and behavioral factors."

For our discussion around PLEs, a clear understanding of communication helps us determine the most effective transmission type to gain the maximum yield for desired outcomes. For example, if you attempt to understand a math equation, verbal communication alone may not be sufficient in the transmission process; it may be more effective to use visual communication shared on-screen with the receiver for discussion.

For a typical use of the word *communication* here, I am referring to how well we can verbally communicate: listen to people; understand them; write, and interpret writing and nonverbal communication; and observe people and infer meaning. Honing these skills, you can be an effective learner, whether it is a one-on-one learning situation or a group environment. Suppose you are having academic difficulty solving a quadratic equation. By being able to communicate verbally or visually what you do not understand, you provide the proper determinates to achieve the desired results-- closing the knowledge gaps. Dr. Munodawafa summed it perfectly, "once knowledge gain is established; it is assumed that the individual will use the knowledge when the need arises or at an opportune time." This is the purpose of self-directed learning.

Technology-enabled learning requires you use your written, verbal, or nonverbal skills, interpret what is being presented, and bring relevant clarity to discussions. These skills are not only important for use within a PLE, but are critical in your personal relationships and associations, academic, and work life situations.

Media, information, and technology literacy have a common link, understanding what these types of literacy are and how they apply to the IL framework. Literacy, as we discuss here, refers to competence or knowledge in a specified area of media, information, and technology and for good measure, we will define what we mean as we want to ensure a common understanding.

Literacy: Media

Media is the communication outlets or tools used to store and deliver information or data. The term refers to components of the mass media communications industry, such as print media, publishing, the news media, photography, cinema, broadcasting, and advertising.

Literacy: Information

Think of information as the resolution of uncertainty; it answers the question of what is an entity . It defines both its essence and the nature of its characteristics. Information has different meanings in different contexts. Thus, the idea becomes related to constraint, communication, control, data, form, education, knowledge, and meaning.

Literacy: Technology

Technology is the sum of techniques, skills, methods, and processes used in the production of goods or services or in the accomplishment of objectives, such as scientific investigation. Systems applying technology by taking an input, changing it according to the system's use, and then producing an outcome are referred to as technology systems or technological systems.

Media literacy, in the context of IL, is our ability to understand the nature and uncertainty of information and the different meanings within different context; this also includes identifying credible sources of information. So why is media literacy important to you and the knowledge process? The better judgment you make about the media sources you incorporate into your learning framework, the more confidence and accuracy you will have in achieving your learning goals.

Ideally, authoritative sources are the most reliable sources of information and learning content. Authoritative sources are considered reliable because they are widely recognized in the field it represents. I will use my own learning experience to demonstrate.

Keeping my technological skills up to date are critical to my success as a learning and development professional. I decided to learn Canvas, a new learning management system (LMS). I can use YouTube to locate Canvas videos authored by many experienced users who create and upload the various functionalities of Canvas for anyone interested or I can choose to use the authoritative source from the company that developed the tool. Canvas is likely to have many videos on every module for their LMS. The advantage I have as a new learner is immediate confidence that any content about the system is accurate. When looking for authoritative sources, look for reliable information providers because its authority or authenticity is widely recognized by experts in the field. This strategy is the essence of using a reliable provider. If you are using a commercial website, carefully assess it for various forms of bias and interest conflicts. For example, if the site is pitching information to lead to their services rather than stating impartial information, find other sites for more neutral and unbiased information. Check to see if the information is current, preferably less than three years old, and consider the author's credentials to lend more credibility.

Moving beyond media sources, the type of information you are seeking must provide the proper context for the type of learning desired. Remember, the definition of information encompassed what an entity is and defines both its essence and nature of its characteristics. For example, if we want to learn what a quadratic equation (the entity) is, the information must convey and describe an entity, idea, or concept providing sufficient information to formulate knowledge and meaning. For our example, Mathsisfun.com cites a quadratic equation as:

"A **quadratic equation** is an **equation** of the second degree, **meaning** it contains at least one term that is squared. The standard form is $ax^2 + bx + c = 0$ with a, b, and c being constants, or numerical coefficients, and x is an unknown variable.[2]"

From that definition, we now have learned that if we see an equation like $4x^2 + 2x + 8 = 0$, we know this type of mathematical entity is a quadratic equation. I promise I will not go nerdy on you, but I wanted to use an example that required us to think about information and how definitions are critical to formulating meaning of an entity or concept. If using the math example has not left you in a fetal position recalling past academic horrors or caused you to throw this book into the nearest trash can, let's move forward and talk about the connection technology has with media and information.

Through the lens of knowledge discovery, applying media and information strategies serves as the basis of sourcing content to meet our learning needs. Technology allows learning opportunities of taking media and information input, changing it according to the learning systems use, and then producing a knowledge or learning outcome.

What is a good example of this? With the PLE platform called G Suite for Education, hosted by Google, and managed by the school, teachers provide students with tools in an online digital environment and students can work together on assignments, collaborate, share experiences, thoughts, and import learning resources which creates a rich peer-to-peer learning experience. This is one example of using technology and media converging to create an empowering learning experience.

Before diving into constructing a PLE, it is worth turning our attention to the concepts of social and collaborative learning and how it informs our experiences within our PLE framework.

3. Social and Collaborative Learning

In the previous chapter, we talked about today's work environment and society, requiring us to solve ambiguous and complex problems which have a direct connection to how we use social and collaborative learning strategies. So, what is social and collaborative learning? Are they one and the same or uniquely different and codependent for learning success? Before answering these questions, let us first understand the framework for social, collaborative, and activities associated with adult learning.

Adult Learning

Andragogy. Now, that is a scholarly word to absorb. In everyday translation, andragogy is a simple way of saying "the art and science of helping adults learn.[1]" Andragogy was defined in 1980 by Malcolm Knowles, famous for his adoption of the theory of andragogy, as an educational term used to distinguish adult learning from teaching children— pedagogy. Pedagogy underscores learner dependency on the teacher for guidance, evaluation, and acquisition of knowledge. To be clear, whether we are talking about adults or children, we use a combination of andragogy and pedagogy in our instruction strategies for adult learners. For example, elementary children require more step-by-step guidance, and while adults may require guidance, they are better equipped to be more self-sufficient. Adult learners generally bring more lived experiences to the learning environment.

When we talk about adult learning processes, we are referring to adults seeking learning assistance, often from individuals who are not educated as teachers. The empowerment of knowledge exploration, *Informal Learning* (IL), offsets the need for teachers from inserting their pedagogical processes rather than allowing the learner to bring their own "natural sequence" to the learning process. These natural sequences of the learning process are characterized by several learning beliefs and characteristics that enable adult learning.

The andragogical expectations believes the nature of adult learners' maturity is driven by self-directness that uses past experiences to learn in the context of current needs that apply to everyday life. The learner assumptions, as described by Malcolm Knowles, include:

- Concept of the learner—moving from "dependency to self-directness.[1]"

- Role of learners' experiences—human growth and experiences accumulate.
- Readiness to learn—learning when it is personally required.
- Orientation to learning--the need to apply what is learned immediately to address competency and performance needs.

Social scientists believe knowledge attainment is situated at a personal level and learning is grounded in the learners' past experiences. Given these assumptions, the framework of Adult Learning Theory (ALT) emphasizes the behavioral aspects of learning and identifies ten characteristics that exist within the context of "community goals and needs.[2]" The following identify behavioral characteristics:

- Problem solving
- Experiential learning
- Empowered self-direction
- Self-correction
- Progressive mastery
- Seeking of meaning
- Critical reflection
- Reciprocal learning

- Interaction with teachers and other learners
- Identifying own learning goals

The behavioral characteristics suggest that the learning process requires more than simply the introduction of topics. A behavioral change needs learners to apply new knowledge in "fresh situations and through active experimentation.[1]" These assumptions are consistent with the concepts of andragogy that suggest that adult learners apply their learning to their "day-to-day lives" as they acquire new knowledge and skills.[1]

The importance of this idea around these behaviors is that in the self-guided process, learners are constructivists--building their own learning world and "new knowledge,"--whereas the learner explores the world and then reflects and critically reviews it to determine whether to accept or reject the new knowledge.[2]

As informal learners, the learning processes are through the crucial basics of meaningfulness and engagement. Meaningfulness is the notion of value--being connected to "self-fulfillment" that is derived in part from personal motivation to produce the learner's positive outcomes.[3] Engagement is defined as the act of acquiring knowledge that is multifaceted and multilayered and includes interaction between other learners or content, stimulating the learner to gain the most benefits from the experience.[3]

The concepts and key assumptions of andragogy provide a basis for analyzing how we frame our thinking about our Personal Learning Environments (PLEs). The concepts and assumptions we have discussed also strengthen the relevant constructs of social learning, activity, and collaboration theories that support our overall approach to building our PLEs. Given this, let us turn our attention to understanding social learning.

Social Learning

Social learning, in theory, is a model highlighting an observational method of transferring behavioral experiences. It specifies that social learning is a recognition, discovery event, or modeling process in which the behavior of another person is the source of learning something new. It is using the power of observational learning from the receiver's belief that the value and behavior being observed is compatible to themselves or "similar other" individuals.[4]

Observation is much more powerful when those modeling behavior or knowledge "encourage learners to articulate what they have observed" in the process.[5]

While observational learning is central to social learning, it is important to emphasize the importance of self-efficacy in its framework. Self-efficacy, through important mastery of new practitioner skills and knowledge and role modeling, goes together with revealing hidden knowledge that must be made accessible to learners and that is best shared in "interconnected communities."[5]

Self-efficacy represents a measure of an individual's confidence in their ability to be successful with complex tasks. Thus, PLEs can serve as valuable approaches to enhancing personal effectiveness and building self-efficacy in professional roles or individual learning endeavors. When we combine collaboration with our learning strategy, it provides opportunities for acting upon what is learned, promotes reflective learning, and integrates into the educational and professional environments.

To further enhance learning, the inclusion of study lessons and demonstration labs enhance your PLE. Today's social learning dynamics are not limited to individual-to-individual learning and the exchange of knowledge; rather, it is reinforced by technology that advances interactions, which links both formal and non-formal learning.

It is important to understand the components of social learning (observation, self-efficacy as a measure of individual confidence, interconnected communities, and role modeling) in the context of the activities you incorporate within your PLE to appreciate the challenges and benefits.

Activity Theory

Activity theory represents one of many frameworks to examine the practices of learning. Activity theory is a "philosophical framework for studying different forms of human praxis as developmental processes, both individual and social levels interlinked at the same time.[6]" In **Figure 2**, the role of activity supports the idea that learning occurs in the context of meaningful activity.

FIGURE 2 Role of Activity Theory

The design of human processes supporting your learning environment should include analysis of the following:

- Examination of the kinds of activities engaged.
- Individuals who are engaging.
- The goals and intentions.
- Objects or products produced.
- Rules and norms defined.
- The community that defines where the activity occurs.

The model represented by these learning activities is consistent with enabling the constructivist nature of your education within your created community. The knowledge you gain can be described as a transformation—a reciprocal event, or a "two-way process of appropriations" that occurs at both the social collective level (in group processes) and at the individual level of interaction and knowledge exchanges.[7] In the context of transformation, learners follow an evolutionary process that starts individually and emerges as a product of "shared worlds of meaning in the process.[7]"

This transformation represents the constructivist orientation, which is interactions of human activity and consciousness in the context of the learners' environment. Ultimately, the learning goal is to transform your lack of knowledge or skills into meaningful knowledge and skills. This kind of individual learning transformation characterizes what can be found in collaborative learning environments that contribute to that success.

Collaboration Theory

Collaboration is a learning method most associated with peer-to-peer situations. Collaboration theory closely aligns with activity theory in that both theories note the reciprocity of knowledge building and skill acquisition that results from shared interests and activities. Our goal of collaborative efforts is aimed at a shared outcome, to reach success that could not be achieved independently. For example, recall the scenario earlier, your boss requested you provide the capability to process running live data points into a machine-learning algorithm. You may require a team effort to accomplish this task. Using the application of collaborative theory, you may pull together a group with deep knowledge of machine learning to run the live data points through the required algorithms. This relationship and collaboration happen in the context of meaningful activities. Think of meaningful activities as deciding what kinds of activities must be addressed by the team to understand what will create a successful learning outcome (refer to "Figure 2: Role of Activity Theory") of the collaborative learning process.

Understanding the collaborative nature of Informal Learning (IL) requires an examination of the practices that support the learning process.

Here are a few specific examples of the collaborative behavior and interactions that learners use to help other learners: experiential learning techniques, observational learning, discussions, and creating processes and procedures that help other learners discover their need to know.

IL's driving factor is derived from our identification and fulfillment of our personal needs.

So, we have taken a quick academic journey to understand key concepts about social and collaborative learning and how adult learning and activity theory intertwine to create a framework. I know you are saying, so now what? What am I supposed to do with all the geek stuff we talked about? It is simple. We will build our PLE in the next chapter.

Summary

Learning, particularly topics that present a challenge , does not have to be accomplished alone. This chapter emphasized the use of social and collaborative learning. You are creating collaboration between those who understand the topic and those seeking to close the knowledge gap. It is these skills you will develop and use within your PLE.

4. Building Your Personal Learning Environment

We began this Informal Learning (IL) journey recalling the cringe-worthy moments in life situations when you felt like the imposter everyone would surely discover. Self-reflection gave way to moments of contemplation of your twenty-first century skills, do I have them? Unceremoniously, you were thrust into adult learning theory for a short burst of academic flashbacks. You have arrived and are now ready to become the IL architect of the knowledge and skills you choose to develop. You are ready to understand how to take the unstructured nature of self-directed learning into a potent tool of success. Embrace your empowerment!

Now you are probably saying to yourself, I am not a teacher or an instructional designer. What do I know about structuring learning to be successful? I know you have seen babies and toddlers in their natural world of discovery. They look at things, hold and manipulate objects, listen to and digest everything you say and do. They are informal learners. You had that natural ability to learn then and you have it now.

The only difference is somewhere along the way some of us relinquished our natural learning abilities and submitted to having knowledge poured into us rather than naturally seeking knowledge. Some of us were lucky enough to retain more of those natural skills. And by no means am I suggesting you start crawling around the room babbling and putting objects in your mouth. What I am suggesting is you still have the foundational inquisitiveness that can be reactivated but in a more sophisticated way.

Surely you have not forgotten those common toddlers' all-time favorite hits, why, how, and where repeated a thousand times daily. Think about it, these simple words are the cornerstone of your inquisitive nature. They lead you down a path of filling in the mental gaps you need to identify and understand things in your world.

In psychology, this process is called creating a schema. A schema is a cognitive structure serving as a framework for building knowledge about people, places, objects, and everything we know. Everything we know is represented by a schema in our minds. Psychologist Cynthia Vinney describes a schema this way:

- A schema is a mental representation that enables us to organize our knowledge into categories.

- Our schemas help us simplify our interactions with the world. They are mental shortcuts that can both help us and hurt us.

- We use our schemas to learn and think more quickly. However, some of our schemas may also be stereotypes that cause us to misinterpret or incorrectly recall information.

- There are many types of schemas, including object, person, social, event, role, and self-schemas.

- Schemas are modified as we gain more information. This process can occur through assimilation or accommodation.

In a nutshell, we are going to combine what we've learned earlier about twenty-first century skills, adult, social and collaborative, and learning activity theories to create a self-constructed environment to meet the knowledge and skills outcomes you need. You control your learning.

Using PLE Platforms and Tools

Before we address Personal Learning Environment (PLE) platforms and tools specifically, having a guide makes it easier to get started.

Your PLE is a combination of tools, people, and services that allow you to construct learning, which becomes the network you build—this is what makes your learning unstructured. You build it in a way that is most meaningful to you. You scale this learning environment to your liking by limiting or expanding the types and number of applications as you see appropriate to meet your needs.

As you consider your PLE, the approach to your model's design has a space that serves as an activity hub, providing your personal working or study setting, and a space where you invite collective activities (network). The areas of activities include:

- **Collection:** gather articles, tools, data, images, and resources
- **Communication:** share ideas, convey information, ask questions, reflect, respond, comment, and clarify
- **Creation:** generate ideas, research, write, create content
- **Collaboration:** synthesize, working with peers, engaging one another

By including the elements described in Figure 3 into your design, you now have a framework to address how you will build your network with tools, resources, and peer collaboration.

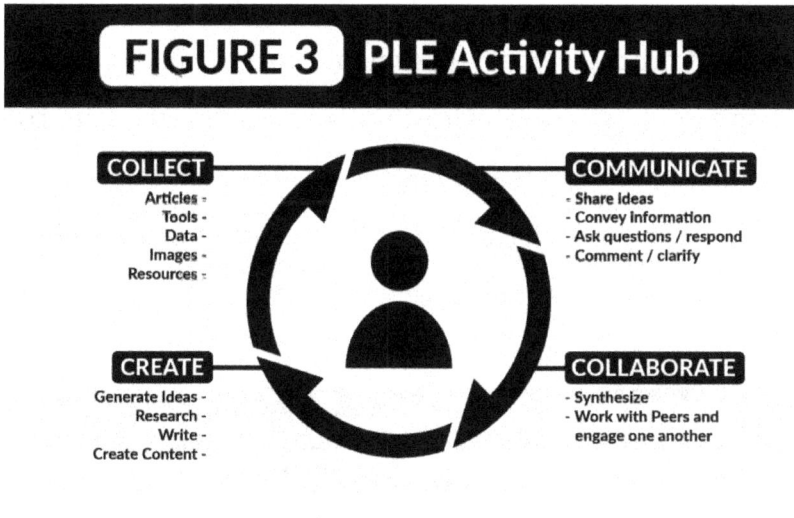

FIGURE 3 **PLE Activity Hub**

COLLECT
Articles -
Tools -
Data -
Images -
Resources -

COMMUNICATE
- Share Ideas
- Convey Information
- Ask questions / respond
- Comment / clarify

CREATE
Generate Ideas -
Research -
Write -
Create Content -

COLLABORATE
- Synthesize
- Work with Peers and
  engage one another

How do I Start Building my PLE?

Examining the Activity Hub, we will build our PLE in stages from Collect, Communicate, Collaborate, and Create elements. Remember, a PLE is not a specific package, rather it is the combination of tools, people, and services that make up individualized resources as an approach to learning. With this in mind, we will create an example PLE with the elements identified in Figure 3.

Collect

Referring to our activity hub, the collect activity will accommodate our ability to collect articles and documents, images, use of tools, and other resources that will be essential to learning a subject or topic of interest. Here is our thought process; what tools might I use to collect articles, images, data, and enable to store, retrieve, manipulate, and share easily? After researching technology tools that provide options you need for this set of activities, you located the follow cloud-based tools:

TABLE 1 Cloud-Based Storage and Collaboration Tools	
Cloud-Based Storage and Collaboration Tools	
DropBox.com	Backblaze
Sync.com	Amazon Drive
pCloud	Microsoft OneDrive
Google Drive	Tresorit
Box	SpiderOak

All these cloud-based tools allow you to upload, transfer, store, and share files with anyone. It allows you to backup and sync documents, photos, videos, and other files to storage and access them from any device no matter where you are. These tools also have advanced sharing features, making it easy to share documents and send files, large or small, to anyone.

Let us assume you have researched all these storage and collaboration tools and decided to select Dropbox because you liked the fact you can have a free account that will work well for you. I recommend searching for free tools as much as possible to determine if they meet your needs before purchasing anything.

Another tool you may consider under the collection activities resources is a learning portal space. Several tools can be found, such as Symbaloo and Combobox. These online sites allow you to create personal start pages where you share your favorite websites or personal homepage with others through social media, email, or shared publicly on their respective application site. Below is an example of the home pages for Symbaloo and Combobox.

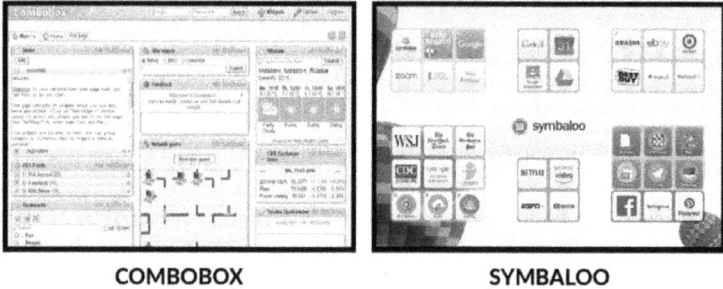

FIGURE 4 Visual Bookmarking Tools

COMBOBOX   SYMBALOO

Imagine having the ability to quickly visit sites like Kahn Academy, LinkedIn, Courser Udemy, or any other resource important to your learning process. You may find that many of these types of tools have features that exists as part of other tools such as Dropbox or perhaps one of these tools may suffice and you decide Dropbox is redundant. Or you may keep both and use for different purposes within your activities. It is all about what works best for you.

Your decision may be based on factors such as free or modest cost or a user-friendly interface. A modest cost may be acceptable and worth paying for to meet your informal learning journey because after all, you are investing in your personal and professional future. I do not support one tool over another, but an interesting feature of some of these tools is the ability to create a learning path and any online material can be used in the lesson plan you create to include videos, articles, quizzes, educational games, and more. Explore and compare various tools and look for robust features that will benefit you.

Communicate and Collaborate

We will discuss communicate and collaborate, as the functional activities are closely related, and the tool must enable our ability to share ideas, convey information, ask questions, respond, comment, and clarify data or other resources. On the surface, it is obvious you can accomplish these activities using email—and you are correct, and while it is extremely limited in capability, it does have a place in your collaborative process. In many ways, communicating and collaborating go together and the relationship of these tools will become clear as they are presented.

Ideally, collaboration can be most effective when you can work on documents jointly with someone, seeing each other enables you to pick up on verbal and visual cues. You can visually demonstrate concepts and methods and so on. Like all technology classes, tools, cost, features, user friendliness, and other factors vary, and collaboration tools are no different. For the sake of our example here, let us assume we have researched several tools and decided to select Zoom as our collaboration choice.

FIGURE 5 Zoom Screen

The most important features for collaboration are face-to-face communication, the ability to share a screen and hand over control, and the whiteboard feature, to name a few. Zoom provides all the necessary features to support your informal learning collaborations, including bringing high-definition video and audio to your meetings that supports up to 1,000 video participants and 49 videos on screen. Multiple participants can share their screens simultaneously and co-annotate for a more interactive session. Filters, reactions, polls, hand raising, and music or video sharing make meetings fun and engaging. Record your meetings locally or to the cloud, with searchable transcripts. You can streamline calendaring of meetings with support from Outlook, Gmail, or iCal. As teams, you can chat with groups, search histories, integrated file sharing, archive files for ten years, and break into one-on-one or group chats.

With these Zoom capabilities, you have the ability to include other people in your learning networks for additional support should you need it. This is our goal, empowering ourselves to shape how our learning happens, independently, or within a group we build.

The final area of the four elements of our PLE activities is Create, identifying the tools we have or will acquire to develop our data and learning content.

Create

Identifying tools and resources to construct our knowledge content outputs and documents is the simplest of the selection processes. Most of the tools we use for this activity are likely familiar: Word, PowerPoint, and Excel. Additionally, tools such as Google Docs, Google Slides, Google Sheets and Snip & Sketch are free. All these tools may have interrelated use with other hub activities we have mentioned to this point. If you have the editing and creation tools you need, you have now completed collecting the resources you need for create your basic PLE. Now, let us take a look at our graphic.

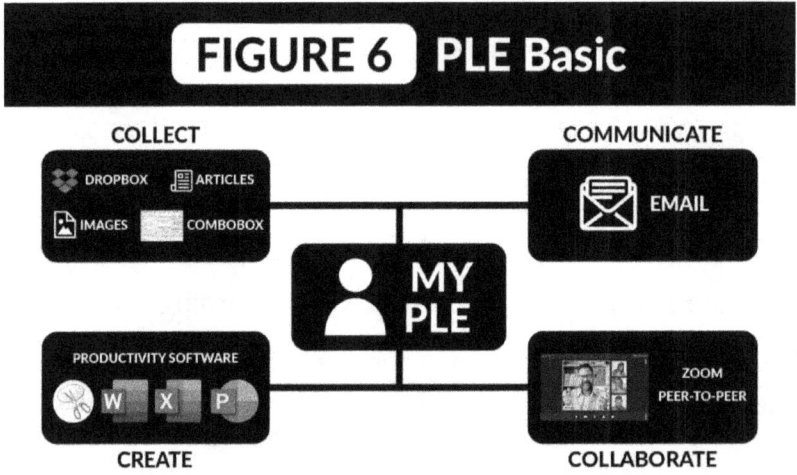

FIGURE 6 PLE Basic

COLLECT

DROPBOX   ARTICLES
IMAGES   COMBOBOX

MY PLE

COMMUNICATE

EMAIL

PRODUCTIVITY SOFTWARE
W X P

CREATE

ZOOM
PEER-TO-PEER

COLLABORATE

The PLE we built now provides us all of the tools for a framework available to mediate our learning. Our PLE is amazingly simple and highly usable to develop our personal learning strategy. As you become more comfortable with building a basic PLE, it can become as simple or intricate as you are comfortable building. Figure 7 is an example of how elaborate some PLEs can become depending on the learner's needs and preference.

FIGURE 7 PLE Complex

As you can see, compared to the PLE in Figure 6, they are not the same, but they accomplish the same goal, providing the framework to advance our knowledge.

Summary

PLEs are a created and customized environment built by and for you. These environments allow you to build schemas, or mental representations, that enable you to learn what you need to understand the world. You create your personal learning environment by using technology and productivity tools to collect, communicate, create, and collaborate resources that enable our self-determined learning needs. Combining these elements, we no longer deal in the abstract. We have a model of learning that can be

Unstructured

graphically depicted and used to expand and modify as needed to further our learning empowerment.

5. HOW DO I DESIGN MY LEARNING?

Now that you have established your Personal Learning Environment (PLE), the next step is to develop your personal instructional strategies, which includes techniques to help you become independent. This is where the power exists because you choose the approach that works best for you.

To be clear, the goal is not to turn you into an instructional designer or your favorite first grade teacher. It is to provide a basic framework about how to think about your learning strategy, allowing your learning to be as unstructured as you please, but enjoying the power of an organized knowledge gaining environment. Combining your learning strategy with your PLE becomes your source of learning empowerment. As with anything we wish to accomplish, we must have a clear direction. We must know what we expect as the result. We call these outcomes "learning objectives" and this is where we will start.

Learning Objectives

How do you benefit from learning objectives? By allowing you to easily understand what you are asking yourself to learn and to be able to demonstrate your new knowledge or skills. They provide you clear learning expectations and help you identify strategies required to be successful. In a nutshell, they identify what is to be learned, how you will demonstrate desired performance, and how that learning will be judged. Here are steps to establish learning objectives.

Step 1. Let your learning objectives begin with something like: "At the conclusion of this activity, I will be able to . . ."

Step 2. Connect Step 1 with an action verb to communicate your performance. The verbs describe an action that are measurable within the teaching timeframe (e.g., you can demonstrate what you have learned).

Step 3. Conclude with the specifics of what you will be doing when demonstrating achievement or mastery of the objectives, including any criterion. Ask yourself, what will be the outcome from the activity?

Example:

Assume you want to learn how to copy a document from a hard drive into a Dropbox folder within three minutes without referencing the instructions. Here is how you might write your learning objective.

`Sample Learning Objective`:

Upon completion of studying the file upload reference instructions for Dropbox, I will be able to:

Copy a document from a hard drive into a Dropbox folder within three minutes without referencing the instructions.

Notice the following breakdown of the learning objective.

- **Observable Action**: Copy a document from a hard drive into a Dropbox folder.

- **Measurable Criteria**: Within three minutes.

- **Conditions of Performance**: Without referencing the instructions.

You may have several learning objectives depending on the topic or subject you want to learn. For our example, we are using one to demonstrate the concept of using learning objectives to help you understand its purpose--

focusing your learning for the desired outcome. Once we have determined what the required learning objectives are, we must decide on the learning strategy. The goal is to connect our learning objectives to the learning strategy.

Learning Strategy

As mentioned earlier, learning strategies are techniques or methods used to accomplish the various learning objectives. Think of them as your blueprint for learning. They facilitate the process of organizing and using a particular set of techniques to learn content more effectively. Essentially, it empowers your learning path for establishing and becoming an independent and strategic learner.

We will present several instructional strategies to help you gain a foothold on developing your own learning discovery process. Remember, there is no right or wrong answer to the strategies you select or design if the outcome meets the objectives you establish. I will present examples of learning strategies and make selections to connect to the learning objective we created earlier. Examples may include:

TABLE 2 Learning Strategies

Learning Strategy	Purpose	Example
Active Reading	Allows learners to remain engaged in the text by using strategies such as read aloud/think aloud, clarifying, summarizing, highlighting, and making predictions. Learners remain focused on what they are reading and increase their ability to comprehend the material.	In a workplace training, participants role-playing peer teaching, debates, and short demonstrations followed by class discussion.
Cooperative Learning	Uses small groups in which learners have roles to accomplish specific tasks and activities. Learners work together to maximize and stimulate their own learning as well as that of others in the group.	In a classroom, students are grouped into small teams so they can discover a new concept together and help each other learn.
Demonstration	Demonstration is a common strategy where learners look at a demonstration by a peer or professor and then apply what they learned to solve a new problem.	The teacher writes a math problem on the whiteboard and solves it step-by-step while explaining how to solve the problem.
Experiential Learning	Experiential learning is the process of learning through experience and is more specifically defined as "learning through reflection on doing." Hands-on learning can be a form of experiential learning and could include learners reflecting on their product as reinforcement.	Rather than reading how to create a paper airplane, a learner experiments building it to determine how to create a paper airplane.

These are just a few examples of learning strategies that may assist your learning efforts. Here are a few more:

Learning Strategy	Purpose	Example
Microlearning	Microlearning deals with relatively small learning units and short-term learning activities. The term is used in e-learning and related fields in the sense of learning processes in mediated environments.	A learner learns how to solve a quadratic equation by focusing on small portions of the entire process of learning how to solve it. For example, one lesson consists of only understanding how to identify a quadratic equations form. $ax^2 + bx + c = 0.$
Prior Knowledge Activation	Encourages learners to connect information they already possess and relate it to the new material they are trying to learn.	A programmer is learning about new features available in a programming language. The programmer uses existing knowledge of the language as a basis of understanding the new features and its capabilities.
Summarization	Use paraphrasing the most important ideas in a text can help to learn. However, this technique only works after students are trained in how to write summaries.	A student, after reading, identifies key words and the main idea and condense important information into their own words during and after reading to solidify meaning of the text.
Technology-Enriched Learning	Enriched learning incorporating active using multimedia and other technology resources. Example Kahn Academy.	Using various technologies like online learning tools and its capability to train users on a topic.

I recommend exploring more instructional strategies to see how they may be useful. As a note of caution, when you search for learning strategies, search authoritative sources as instructional strategies, and you will find they are described from the context of teacher or instructional designers. You simply need to understand them in the viewpoint of what they are doing and apply them to your learning efforts.

We have a few examples of learning strategies identified above, now we need to connect some of these strategies to the learning objectives of the topic or subject we chose to learn. Recall our learning objective earlier.

I will be able to:

Copy a document from a hard drive into a Dropbox folder within three minutes and without referencing the instructions document.

Observable Action: Copy a document from a hard drive into a Dropbox folder.

Measurable Criteria: Within three minutes.

Conditions of Performance: Without referencing the instructions.

Given our learning objective, let us say you have decided the best learning strategy to copy a document from a hard drive into a Dropbox folder is to use **Experiential Learning** and **Technology Enriched Learning** in a collaborative way to learn this task. How does this fit with the PLE we built? Let's revisit the PLE as designed.

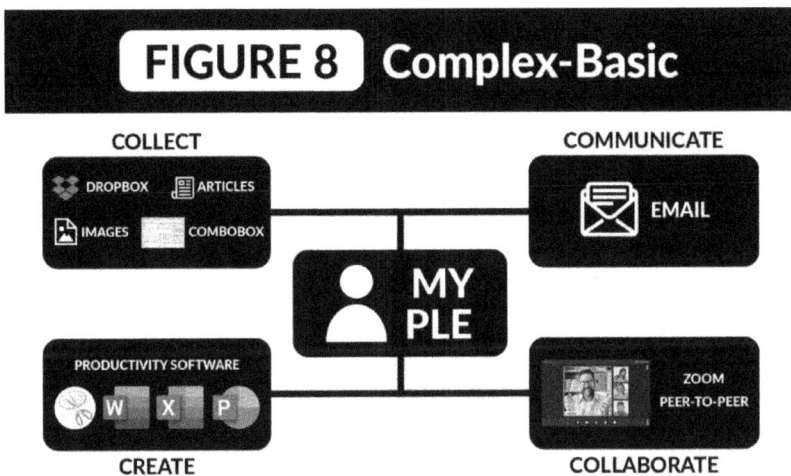

FIGURE 8 Complex-Basic

Within our PLE structure, we have the tools needed to address our current learning tasks. Using Zoom, which is part of our PLE, John decides he will work with Mary, who is struggling with the concept of copying files to Dropbox.

John shares his learning objective with Mary, who thinks the objectives are perfect to accomplish their learning activity. Communicating with Mary on Zoom, John and Mary share their computer screens and they can watch a tutorial on YouTube that demonstrates a step-by-step visual and verbal presentation or study the Dropbox reference guide on how to copy a file from a computer hard drive to a Dropbox folder. After observing and listening, John and Mary felt comfortable enough to experiment (experiential learning). After each created a folder in Dropbox , John and Mary experimented by having the step-by-step list on screen available to follow the process for the upload from their computers.

John and Mary successfully completed the document upload task. John says to Mary, "Let's see if we can do this task without the step-by-step instructions available on screen in three minutes." The three minutes without reference documents are part of their learning objective criteria. John and Mary set a timer and repeated their attempt to upload a different document into their Dropbox folders without referring to the step-by-step instructions. Both completed the task in 90 seconds successfully. John and Mary met their learning objective!

This is a simple example, but the purpose is to demonstrate how we connect learning objectives and strategies to apply our learning on our PLE framework and design our schema.

Understanding the schema, as discussed earlier, we can readily grasp the importance of building a knowledge acquisition framework that allows us to connect our learning objectives and strategies, ultimately creating success in our learning journeys and self-empowerment.

Summary

Building a PLE is important and having a strategy to learn within the model is equally important. Knowing what you want to learn must be converted into learning objectives which are measurable as demonstrated with the given example. Your verification of learning is your ability to accomplish the task or demonstrate the learning you set out to achieve. The reward of this new learning is the addition of new schema or knowledge into your long-term memory to recall with confidence when you need it.

6. Coaching and Mentoring

This chapter redirects our attention beyond the elements of tools, technology, and an assortment of artifacts and will integrate the human element through the lens of coaching and mentoring as a constructive piece of Informal Learning (IL) success. The discussion around coaching and mentoring is brief, but I believe the topic is worthy of consideration as you think about the Personal Learning Environment (PLE) components you construct.

Coaching

What is the relevance of coaching to you as an informal learner? I do not mean coaching in the sports sense. Instead I am suggesting coaching to help learners increase their knowledge and skills using an experienced person, "the coach," to achieve a specific personal or professional goal by providing training and guidance. Using a coach is not a requirement for your PLE's success. Some will find adding a coach beneficial, and others not so much, but it is an option to which you decide the value. A coaching relationship in the context of its corporate use, an employee fails to accomplish tasks as expected and assigned a coach to shore up the requisite skills.

In the context of IL, think of coaching as a process that aims to improve your knowledge and skills focused on the "here and now" to achieve what you need. A coaching relationship does not have to be a formal structure where you meet with someone weekly for six weeks or even a month. It could be a minute-by-minute engagement if that is all needed. I would like you to view coaching as a just-in-time approach to meet specific learning needs.

You are learning informally; make any incorporated coaching align with this strategy. For simplicity, let us go back to the math example of the quadratic equations. The purpose of coaching, even in an informal manner, requires connecting with a coach who is experienced or has expertise in a particular area. In this case, someone with a high degree of competency with math and who understands quadratic equations. During your learning about quadratic equations on Kahn Academy, a part of your PLE structure, you are doing fine. Still, you run into an area you cannot figure out because of a concept you have not been able to understand.

You were wise enough before starting your learning tasks on Kahn Academy to anticipate you may need a little math coaching assistance and wanted to identify a potential coach before you required it. You remembered your friend

Paul loves math and it is his favorite subject. You contact Paul, and he agrees to be your just-in-time math coach. That moment has come, and you hit that problem learning how to solve a quadratic equation. You reach out to Paul via email and say, "Hey Paul, I've run into a snag learning to solve quadratic equations, do you have a moment to connect on Zoom?" Paul connects with you on Zoom, which is a resource within your PLE. You share your computer screen with Paul, showing him your lesson and discuss your challenges. Paul walks you through the equation and explains where you went wrong and clarifies the concept in a way you can better understand.

By sharing your computer screen and allowing camera access for you and Paul to view each other, Paul can determine if you understand through watching your body language and discussion. I think you get the point, and I hope you caught the pattern related to developing a PLE, all the resources you needed were there as support.

The key message is the value of coaching is only as valuable as you determine it to be. Knowing your strengths and weaknesses determines the best resources, even if it does not included coaching.

Mentoring

One of the most confusing relationships to many is the interaction of coaching versus mentoring and there is a distinct difference between the two. Coaching is more performance-driven, designed to improve the professional's on-the-job performance. Mentoring is more development-driven, looking not just at the professional's current job function but beyond, taking a more holistic approach to career development. We talk about mentoring from a professional career context, but mentoring can and is used in academic and other settings. The Center for Corporate and Professional Development at Kent State University suggests that mentoring should be used to:

- Motivate talented professionals to focus on their career/life development.
- Inspire individuals to see what is possible in their career/life.
- Enhance the professional's leadership development.
- Transfer knowledge from senior to junior professionals.
- Broaden intercultural or cross-cultural ties within the organization.

- Use the mentoring process as an entree to succession planning.

Whether we are talking about coaching or mentoring, relationships is at the heart of both approaches. The relationships we build with the people who engage with us in mentoring or coaching journeys directly determines its success or failure. The Center for Corporate and Professional Development also suggests that mentoring should be used to:

- **Trust and respect your coach or mentor.** Every meaningful relationship is built on the foundation of trust and respect. You must trust your coach or mentor to provide you with expert guidance, feedback, and support based on his/her life experiences. Respect his/her opinions and ideas because your coach or mentor has lived through challenges you may not have yet experienced.

- **Establish ground rules.** Determine how often you will meet, how long your relationship will last, outline of roles, importance of confidentiality, and preferred methods of communication and feedback.

- **Determine your outcome.** What do you want to have happen to you at the end of the relationship? Discuss this with your coach or mentor.

Establishing a coaching or mentoring relationship requires locating the right individuals willing to serve in these roles. You may know individuals interested in serving as your coach or mentor. If not, there is no time like the present to start developing a good network of individuals with expertise in the areas essential to serve as your mentor or coach. Professional networking sites like LinkedIn, among others, represent one of the largest and most common social and learning network sites. Should you decide to use coaching or mentoring as part of your learning strategy, add it to your PLE framework by updating your visual graphic to include all the elements of your PLE.

Earlier, we created our PLE that did not include coaching, mentoring, and social networks. Our PLE graphic below, reflects incorporating these elements ("Social Platforms and "Mentoring/Coaching").

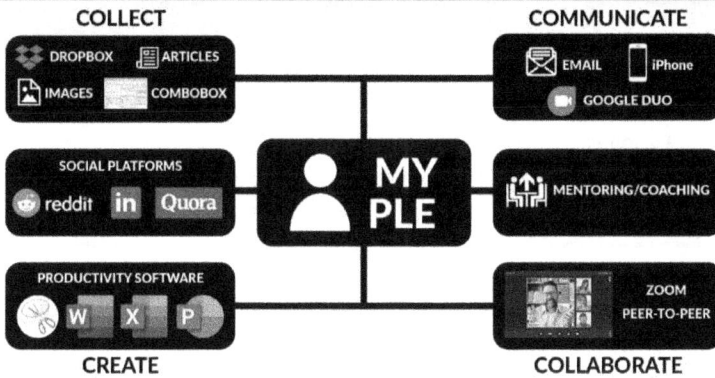

FIGURE 9 — Expanded PLE – Coaching]/Mentoring

COLLECT

DROPBOX   ARTICLES

IMAGES   COMBOBOX

SOCIAL PLATFORMS

reddit   in   Quora

PRODUCTIVITY SOFTWARE

W   X   P

CREATE

MY PLE

COMMUNICATE

EMAIL   iPhone

GOOGLE DUO

MENTORING/COACHING

ZOOM
PEER-TO-PEER

COLLABORATE

It is worth noting that coaching and mentoring, like other elements of our PLE example, have an overlapping relationship with other features. Adding mentoring and coaching to your framework as identified in the graphic Figure 6: PLE Basic, requires a decision about how we plan to communicate and track information and the relationship with the coach or mentor. What will the tool be used for this? Looking at our current PLE Resources, we can make the following decisions.

TABLE 3	PLE Resources
PLE Resources	**Coaching/Mentoring Activity**
Social Platform	Network source for connecting with a coach or mentor.
Dropbox	Shared Coach/Mentor Dropbox folder. Store Coach/Mentor contact information, all documents and resources related to coaching and mentoring sessions.
Zoom	Use to have coaching or mentoring face-to-face virtual sessions.
Email	Use for routine communications with the coach or mentor.
iPhone	Store coach or mentor phone number and other information.

As with learning objectives discussed earlier, everything we do to further our journey is associated with the PLE framework and coaching and mentoring are no exceptions.

Many people associate coaching and mentoring as limited to the affiliation with businesses, and while they are most likely to be used within them, nothing prevents you from creating a coaching or mentoring arrangement that benefits your personal or professional growth. Remember, your goal is to develop a PLE through the collection of resources that enables your ability to learn what you want, when you want, and how you want.

Summary

Learning does not have to be accomplished in isolation. Increasing your learning and empowerment sometimes requires building relationship such as coaching and mentoring. As with building a PLE, it is your choice to select beneficial coaches and mentors.

7. CONNECTING INFORMAL LEARNING TO FORMAL STRUCTURES

Embrace the need for life-long learning opportunities as the bridge over your learning obstacles. A blend of informal and formal learning opportunities can form the foundation for individual success in life, career progression, and personal growth.

Informal Learning (IL) is increasingly a necessity to boost formal learning structures to extend knowledge by using new and emerging social technologies, bringing together communities of similar interests, and fostering learning that is reactive to situational needs. The reality is IL is critical in a rapidly changing society.

We are fortunate to live in a technology-enhanced world that enables and empowers us to convert IL's unstructured nature into a combination of various forms of learning relationships, networks, and communities. As your knowledge and understanding of self-learning increases, put it into action, dare to imagine the possibilities of success with acquiring new knowledge by being the architect of your learning.

Being an Advocate for Your Learning

One can find countless education and training programs, and some common types include:

- General Educational Development (GED) programs
- Postsecondary Degrees (associate, bachelor, or graduate)
- Professional Certification
- On-The-Job Training
- Military Training
- Corporate Training and Universities
- Extension Schools
- English as a Second Language
- Personal Development and Self-Paced Learning
- Voluntary Services Training
- Industry Associations and Conferences

The commonality of these programs and their respective curriculums is the teacher-focused direct instruction methodology. Direct instruction refers to how the instructional delivery is structured, sequenced, and led by an instructor with presentations, lectures, and some demonstrations. Content is directed at students rather than holistically engaging them; thus, content "directed at students" is a traditional method that is not student-centered. Applying a lecture-style method too extensively may not be in the best interest of a class full of passive learners who take notes, particularly those who may be struggling with a topic and reluctant to express their lack of understanding in a lecture-style environment. This does not mean there is no place for a lecture, the question is whether there is room to allow for a diverse approach to delivering content? There must be.

Ideal instructional strategies, from a learner-centric approach, is that the method of instructional delivery allows flexible learning. It is not good enough that the teachers' learning strategies work for 70 percent of the classroom. Studies have shown that many children are not successful because of the amount and type of instruction needed. Children, like adults, have different learning preferences. Educators must strive to address the learning needs to the maximum number of learners as possible. Imagine if, from an instructional context, we educated our children to use casual learning and how to engage peers, selected resources, and yes, educators for their own success—that's empowerment.

These actions may lessen the sole responsibility and dependence on educators, strengthening the students' learning capabilities.

You may be saying to yourself, I have no control of the instructional strategy a teacher selects, what can I do? Here is where I want you to pause and reconsider your thinking about how powerless you perceive yourself in a learning environment. Become your own advocate for your challenges. Being intimidated by educational professionals is self-defeating. If you embrace the concepts and find it works for you, be a proponent for change by requesting and collaborating with educators to broaden their instructional strategies to incorporate non-formal learning within their curriculum.

Collaborating with educators is particularly important for parents who have children in the K-12 systems who may be disadvantaged by the system's power dynamics. If your child consistently fails to meet learning requirements, it may suggest existing instructional approaches are not adequate to meet your child's needs. To be fair, there may be other potential factors contributing to the learning challenges that may need to be explored. Still, it is worthy to determine if the instructional strategies within the classroom are the root cause before looking for other potential causes.

For adults in educational systems, take ownership by having a one-on-one conversation with your instructor about the classroom teaching strategies. Take responsibility to know whether educators are familiar with methods of self-directed learning that will help your learning. It is highly likely they have varying degrees of familiarity and can incorporate it into their curriculum. As someone who has taught accounting in community college systems, I always have appreciated students who take the initiative, making me aware that they do not understand accounting concepts. It enabled me to modify my teaching strategies to accommodate my students' unique learning preferences and incorporate IL strategies. Nothing in the classroom has ever made me smile more than to see the reaction and sense of accomplishment on a student's face, and exclaiming "I got it!"

Will all educators be receptive to feedback requesting the incorporation of non-traditional teaching methodology? I would like to think so, but some educators will not apply it for whatever reason. The beauty is, a non-receptive educator does not have control over you deciding to build your PLE to meet your specific learning needs. As discussed in Chapter 4, you have the power to create your learning environment and connect with subject matter experts, online content, and other learners who may be struggling. Use your creative energy, PLE, and resources to give you the learning edge you need for success. When challenged by a lack of non-traditional learning strategies in a formal system, creating your PLE is what I mean by connecting IL to traditional structures.

One way or the other, self-guided learning can be added to the teacher's instructional strategy, by taking the initiative to construct your PLE, or it may be a combination of both. The question is, are you motivated enough to create a win-win situation?

In today's educational systems, it is becoming common to find the creation of online communities within classrooms. Technology has opened new opportunities of meaningful learning avenues for knowledge building to facilitate the processes of non-formal learning in a rapid knowledge economy.

This book was written during the COVID-19 pandemic. Educational institutions were forced to re-examine their use of technology and instructional strategies and learning communities. In the educational space, this is like corporate communities of practices, which are environments where participants share an interest in a mutual domain for collective learning. Online IL has become most notable as learning communities for professional associations seeking to provide peer-to-peer knowledge and engagement. Given the proliferation of technology, online learning resources, and peer-to-peer platforms, online environments have now created an interwoven experience of formal and self-directed learning. Motivated students, business professional, self-directed learners, and entrepreneurs can use informal tools to learn new skills, acquire new knowledge, develop their sense of student or professional identity, and use social networking opportunities to explore and learn the complexities of their roles. Learning communities are characterized as:

- They are self-organizing.
- Their members learn together by engaging in learning activities and discussions.
- There is a shared "collection of experiences, stories, best practices, and ways of solving problems.[1]"

The guiding principle of communities of learning, as we will refer to them here, is the idea that knowledge-oriented learning is supported by members who bring a level of competence from their shared educational or professional domain. In learning communities, users employ their autonomy to pursue goals and strategies that meet their individual needs. Online communities represent a practitioner orientation for knowledge building, adding to the dynamics of how learning communities function within online environments. The success or failure of learning communities, even within the PLE you build, depends on whether members work together in virtual groups, develop strategies for getting to know one another, create strategies to studies or work-based learning, and develop effective communication strategies. Understanding these concepts are important when considering how you create your PLE. It is easy to see how the PLE we built in preceding chapters has relevance to educational systems as a component of our current non-formal structures.

Here is what our updated PLE looks like adding an educational system. Notice that we have added "Education System" to the graphic in **Figure 10: PLE - Education System.**

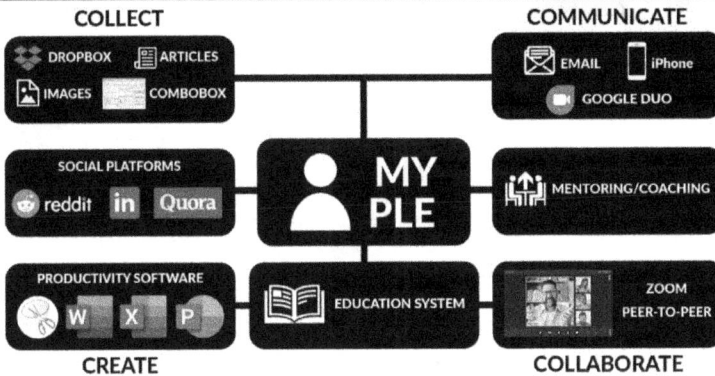

FIGURE 10 Expanded - PLE Education System

COLLECT
- DROPBOX
- ARTICLES
- IMAGES
- COMBOBOX

COMMUNICATE
- EMAIL
- iPhone
- GOOGLE DUO

SOCIAL PLATFORMS
- reddit
- in
- Quora

MY PLE

MENTORING/COACHING

PRODUCTIVITY SOFTWARE
- W
- X
- P

EDUCATION SYSTEM

ZOOM
PEER-TO-PEER

CREATE

COLLABORATE

What impact does this have on our PLE design? Essentially, there is no measurable impact. The design says that in addition to having a PLE with the previous components, we are now using it to learn what we need to in a formal learning structure such as school. All the tools and resources associated with the previous PLE design is now used for school, the same way the PLE will be used to learn other topics that may not be part of an educational system. All the topics or subjects you are learning in a school, where you may be experiencing learning challenges, follow the same self-designed learning approaches discussed in Chapters 2-6. We could add another component for our professional, such as work environment; the same concepts and strategies apply.

This chapter's central theme relates to modifying your PLE to accommodate formal learning structures. These traditional learning environments may include school, work, workforce development, job skills programs, college, university, or professional development, and identifying individualized learning needs—knowing your reasons and motivations to learn to strengthen your knowledge skills. The learning environments in themselves are not what is important. Effectively using IL and personal learning strategies are what matter.

Summary

Connecting the formal learning environments like school or work-based training is not intended to create learning from scratch but is an extension of your learning process to use your PLE to close a given knowledge gap. Think of it like having a tutor except you are the tutor who has built a model to meet your learning needs.

8. CREDIT FOR INFORMAL LEARNING IN THE WORKPLACE

The increased importance of Informal Learning (IL) on employee performance requires reexamination within the corporate sectors. Within these environments, the growing awareness of how adults continually gain new skills and knowledge outside of formal learning requires understanding the choice and value of engaging in independent learning. Employee learning activities must go beyond the immediate needs of corporate strategic goals and compliance requirements.

For businesses awakening to the value of personal learning in the work environment, the revelation typically limits itself to resources within their technology domains' firewalls. Given the security risks of cyber attacks such as phishing and other data breaches, allowing individuals to pull external resources from outside corporate firewalls is understandable. However, even the limited application of self-guided learning that may exist does not go the distance, particularly when it comes to formally recognizing the gain individuals achieve through resolving their knowledge gaps on the job. Your goal should include gaining formal credit for employee self-driven learning in performance reviews and human resources records—your empowerment.

If you are familiar with corporate learning management systems (LMSs)or instructor-led training, the learning content accomplishes organizational needs; general learning and training are generic to all employees. Sure, there is usually a catalog of other general skills or courses provided by their third-party LMS vendor, but have you ever searched for content specifically targeted to represent your gap in knowledge or skills and nothing met those needs? It is this space that underlies the foundation and reason for IL.

Imagine all the elements of knowledge acquisition we discussed earlier. Our focus here is about showing targeted self-development, specifically, having your learning endeavors validated as part of your organization's performance considerations.

How would you create a workplace scenario to have your employer appreciate and value self-learning efforts as part of your performance and development goals?

As an example, assume Katherine, an administrative assistant, has become fascinated with her Database Administrators (DBA) colleagues' role. Katherine has a general idea of what her colleagues do, but is interested in building skills to shift into a DBA role. She must begin with a plan that will allow her knowledge and skills to transition into entry-level DBA work as part of her longer-term goals. Katherine must first understand the DBA job role and core tasks. As part of her initial research, she may have conversations with her colleagues to discuss how they got their start.

Additionally, she may determine what skills employers seek to get a perspective from the employer context; it may be helpful to seek job descriptions as the basis of figuring out where your independent learning should start and crafting your strategy.

Look at a job role in its entirety. Table 4 is an example of crucial job roles and responsibilities. Give thought to how you would start crafting a learning strategy before examining how Katherine approached it.

Below is an example of key job role and responsibilities of a typical DBA.

TABLE 4 Database Administrator Job Role	
General Job Tasks	**Sample Tasks Description**
Installation, configuration, upgrade, and migration	Installs hardware, various software, and operating systems on servers.
Backup and recovery	Implements, and periodically test backup and recovery plans for the databases they manage.
Database security	Understands security models that a database product uses and how to use it effectively to control access to the data. The three basic security tasks are authentication (setting up user accounts to control logins to the database), authorization (setting permissions on various parts of the database), and auditing (tracking who did what with the database)

Based on discussions in previous chapters, are you confident you can build your learning for a specific DBA function? Let us see how Katherine approached it.

General Job Tasks	**Sample Tasks Description**
Storage and capacity planning	Plans how much disk storage will be required and monitors available disk space are key DBA responsibilities. Watching growth trends to advise management on long-term capacity plans.
Performance monitoring and tuning	Uses various tools, and monitors database servers on a regular basis to identify bottlenecks (parts of the system that are slowing down processing) and remedy them.
Troubleshooting	Assess database server problems and understands how to quickly correct issues without losing data or making the situation worse.

Now that Katherine has researched and understood the core and general tasks performed by a DBA, she is ready to put together her Individual Learning Plan (ILP). Katherine has good computer skills but knows that is not enough.

Based on her self-assessment of her knowledge and skills, Katherine decides a good starting point is learning "Installation, Configuration, and Upgrade, and Migration" described below.

Installation, configuration, upgrade, and migration. Although system administrators generally are responsible for the hardware and operating system on a given server, installation of the database software is typically up to the DBA. This job role requires knowledge of the hardware prerequisites for an efficient database server and communicating those requirements to the system administrator. The DBA then installs the database software and selects from various options in the product to configure it for the purpose it is being deployed. As new releases and patches are developed, it is the DBA's job to decide which are appropriate and to install them. If the server is a replacement for an existing one, it is the DBA's job to transfer the data from the old server to the new one.

Katherine determined, through self-assessment, she needs the following knowledge and skills:

- What a server is and how it functions.
- Installing database software and selecting options for deployment.

- Migrating data from an old to a new server.

This assessment yields the basis of Katherine's Individual Learning Plan (ILP). Within that, Katherine can now build all the elements we discussed in Chapter 5, her learning objectives, learning strategies, and using them in her Personal Learning Environment (PLE).

What does this look like in practice? The ILP does not have to be complicated; it can be as simple or complex as you like. I prefer simplicity. Below is an example of a simple ILP.

FIGURE 11 Individual Learning Plan

Name:	Date Implemented:
Purpose of Informal Learning:	
Learning Objectives:	
Learning Strategy	
Criteria for Success (Validation):	
Manager Approval: _____	Approved SME: _____
SME Validation:	
Signature _____	Date: _____

This simple ILP has all the necessary information that outlines a potential plan to carry out your learning goals successfully. It provides a basis for a collaborative conversation with your manager about your learning goals and a discussion about who may be appropriate to serve as a subject matter expert (SME), mentor, or coach to validate your knowledge gain within the organization.

Success must occur in collaboration with the identified SME based on the learning objectives. Work with your SME to determine how he or she will validate your knowledge and skills. Perhaps the criteria may be some combination of oral discussion, written, or practical demonstrative methods of proving your knowledge and skills--it is a collaborative joint decision process.

Validation of your knowledge and skills is your primary goal in the process. As an essential element of verification by the SME, in this case, the selection of an experienced DBA will validate the knowledge and skills based on your learning objectives and agreed-upon criteria. The SME's signature on the ILP form assures your manager you have successfully learned the knowledge or effectively demonstrated mastery of skills identified.

Once Katherine has completed her ILP for the DBA tasks, she can repeat the process for the remaining general job responsibilities she identified. This strategy serves as a basis for perhaps connecting these newly developed skills to an entry-level certification. For example, Microsoft offers an entry-level certification for a database. The basic level certification presents a broad scope of central ideas and is a prerequisite for the associate level.

The best advocate for your professional development and empowerment is *you*. You may have to educate your manager on the purpose and value of IL and how you are using it to enhance your current knowledge and learn other critical skills to contribute to personal and company success. IL is relatively new in many organizations and that is OK. This is your opportunity for self-empowerment.

Managers typically have a great deal of latitude concerning assisting and guiding employees in professional development and training. Use this opportunity wisely by incorporating IL into your annual training and professional development. Your efforts may also be an excellent opportunity to encourage your manager to work with senior leadership to promote the implementation of IL more broadly across the organization. Should your organization have the chance to experience the value and ease of using IL, it may become a norm and benefit others. Share what you have learned with your peers, help them become successful. The more you share your personal learning experiences, the more likely your organization will catch wind of these successes and emulate your manager's decision to incorporate IL into your performance records. It could spark your manager to realize an opportunity for human resources to educate and train other managers across the company about providing employees the opportunity to incorporate self-guided learning into their performance reviews.

I have been in corporate training and development for more than 20 years. My experience has shown me a clear need for self-designed and empowered learning success within organizations. Encouraging employees to engage and use IL and development structures is a win-win benefit for the organization and the employee. The organization gains a greater understanding of individuals' need to combine them with its required training to create a more holistic and dynamic learning organization.

Some training professionals argue we must find a way of formalizing the unstructured nature of IL, while others say that defeats the purpose. I am not a proponent of formalization as it may lead to the learning process being less "learner-centric." Integrating IL is not to provide another opportunity for organizations to focus on its needs. It should be merged and directed by the learner as we have described throughout the book, and through the example of Katherine learning DBA knowledge and skills. The organization must allow learners to maintain autonomy to maintain the unstructured and natural learning elements that are essential. The only exception and connection of a formality is the validation of knowledge and skills they must attest.

Educate your organization on your IL application . Once you have mastered the processes, why not give your peers presentations through learning sessions using collaboration tools? Create forums and discussion groups to explore job-based self-learning for skills and knowledge building and create learning networks. Encourage others to investigate what this type of empowerment is and how to use it to their advantage.

Summary

Today's workplace is an ever-changing environment where the tools and knowledge required for success are never static. Nothing is more evident than the technology and systems we see companies instituting to meet their needs. With change comes the potential for opportunity. Many of us recognize that if we learn other tools and systems within the workplace it may position us for personal growth and promotion, and sometimes even job survival. Company-sponsored training should not be the only recognized instruction in your performance reviews. Do not be intimidated to advocate for a formal acknowledgment of the individual learning you have achieved that benefits you and your company. Use the process described in this chapter to present your ILP to your company with confidence. Execute your plan-and feel the empowerment!

9. THE FUTURE OF INFORMAL LEARNING

Informal Learning (IL) is not new. There is an ongoing renaissance as it becomes more commonplace and increasingly gaining traction as essential to the role it plays in education and training strategies, and a necessity to just-in time individualized learning needs. Knowledge and skills attainment in a highly technical and knowledge-based economy is a crucial driver to personal success. Education and training professionals continue to acknowledge the importance of IL, notably for the future of corporate learning and development, K-12 education, college and post-graduate studies, personal enrichment, and even entrepreneurial skill-based endeavors. IL's role is a logical connection to a world increasingly anchored in technology and requires flexible and self-organizing structures to supplement formal learning.

Businesses and educational institutions may significantly benefit from examining their organizations' learning structures, creating a blend of formal and non-traditional opportunities. Yet, formal learning remains the dominant approach for training employees.

Companies, including educational institutions, often hire contract instructional designers to develop training programs and content tailored to their needs. Contract, or freelance, instructional designers are temporary personnel used to supplement regular employees.

Freelancers face enormous pressure to continually build the knowledge required to do their jobs due to the expectations they face in the complex organizations they work with and because of on-going technology changes. My research participants, who were instructional designers, described the ability to self-educate as critical to their success. When asked about the future direction of IL and the relationship to formal learning in their profession, their responses revealed a belief that the future will blend traditional and non-traditional. As one participant stated, "I think there is going to be more emphasis on IL because . . . there are more technologies and tools available to help." Another participant predicted it will grow tremendously as there has been a big paradigm shift and referenced IL as a good thing versus the standalone brick and mortar classroom training as the only option.

All research participants indicated their future success depends on expanded opportunities for controlling one's own learning. They cited the need to create knowledge-building communities, maintain organic learning opportunities beyond formal structures, and sharpen future skills for those who have been out of traditional training for some time.

Contracted instructional designers gather the information they need about the organization, and identify subject matter content that may not be part of their knowledge base. So here is the question: if a self-learning strategy is a key to their professional success, why wouldn't it be crucial to *your* success?

Imagine the transformational power of instructional designers and educators who are focused on learning how to learn as part of their mission. What a gift of personal empowerment that would be for learners in organizations! I think instructional designers' future roles will include pursuing more in-depth knowledge about IL as a skill that learners must develop to bridge the gap between formal and non-formal strategies.

K-12 and higher education environments already embrace online learning as a viable means of educating, manifested in the instructional strategies they use. One caveat for online learning and its effectiveness is the grade level of implementation—it may not be as effective with early elementary grades. Young children require a stricter pedagogical approach to learning than adults. But when properly integrating IL, we gain empowered learners with the same success as the instructional designers. For example, Khan Academy and other content producers provide thousands of free course offerings that support students who run the gamut from elementary to doctoral students. The learning efforts around this delivery method are at the heart of what IL is all about—no educators are sitting with the learner; it is self-driven learning that often supplements content taught in classrooms.

Higher education institutions have fully embraced online learning as a path to the degrees they offer. Online college courses require learners to be highly motivated and self-driven to be successful and it plays a significant role in the process of self-learning. No spontaneous feedback loops when challenged with the learning content compared to face-to-face learning—quickly raising your hand and asking the teacher for clarification to what may not be understood. Thus, it is important to have a reliable Personal Learning Environment (PLE) to address learning needs.

For collegiate institutions, the extent to which they are open to validating IL in a meaningful way comes into focus.

In terms of a meaningful way, I am referring to reducing the number of required course credits in a curriculum if individuals can test out of courses. For example, if you have used IL to tackle a class's subject matter, you should attempt to test out rather than spending valuable time and money on a semester or quarter course. I know the skeptic will say that is a revenue tactic of institutions and they will never allow cutting the number of courses in a degree program, but it may surprise you to know there are programs that will allow you to test out of classes. The College Board (clep.collegeboard.org) has many courses tested through the College-Level Examination Program (CLEP) exams. Appendix B: College-Level Examination presents a list of exams by category that CLEP uses as a testing-out method for college credit.

So why is this information important? Recall IL's original intent —empowering you to construct learning how, when, and under what conditions you desire. Your efforts to build a PLE and using all the techniques we discussed in Chapter 5 are your tools for success. It will enable your educational or personal learning goals, particularly if you have been out of the academic system for years. Using a PLE for your educational purposes lessens feeling intimidated by the classroom.

We touched on the topic of technology briefly through the research participants identifying its increased use. Still, I would be remiss to omit the discussion through the lens of social technology as an integral part. Social technology, from the premise that in "today's digital world, technology breaks barriers of space, time, and or presence or absence of mediators.[1]" For example, my research indicated that contract instructional designers used social media tools and platforms such as YouTube, LinkedIn, Google, Reddit forums, and many other sources. Educators and instructional designers have opportunities to explore self-imposed knowledge building in an age of social connection through technology, and so should you.

The goal of this book has been to inspire you about using learning constructs, expressly by taking advantage of IL's unstructured nature. To combine varied resources (such as other people, new technology, social platforms, personal research, and collaboration) and to acquire the knowledge you need to be successful in any endeavor, whether applying it to day-to-day work or entrepreneurial endeavors.

Learners, educators, and business leaders should recognize that IL's unstructured and individualized nature requires support, not a restriction, from outside the learner: provide resources, particularly social learning technology that enables IL to occur naturally through the people, technology, and applications the learner deems best; understand that informal learners aren't the same in their learning styles and processes; recognize that IL is considered the foundation of learners' success and casual approach learning is a consistent future fixture in the learning process and not a current trend.

IL and its benefits can enhance the full spectrum of learning opportunities when individuals control their knowledge, permitting them to determine what they need to learn, when they need to know it, and how they choose to pursue it. It has an exciting future if the field of instruction embraces its individualized, unstructured nature.

As I participate in professional social networking and learning environments such as LinkedIn, I am encouraged to witness individuals' ongoing accomplishments completing their educational journeys later in life. Finding not only their own Rosetta Stone to learning and newfound career success, but openly discussing the challenges of education and how it impacted their lives and reasons for seeking a second life in the educational space. Their motives are many; some to fight the past demons that made them believe learning challenges could not be overcome. For some, it is about demonstrating and setting examples for their children. No matter the reason, people are increasingly interested in finding guidance and frameworks that help them learn. As we continue to employ online learning, remote work proliferates and requires job skills and knowledge to evolve rapidly. Its use has opened the door to those without formal degrees to obtain life success—not everyone wants to go to college. Does this mean they cannot be successful? No. Take the case of Bill Gates; he does not have a college degree.

Bill "enrolled at Harvard College in 1973 to study pre-law but also studied mathematics and took a graduate-level computer science course. Gates left Harvard after two years, opting instead to start his own computer software company.[1]" Brice, a friend I met in the work environment, is another example of the power of self-learning and an exceptional learner. Brice is what professionals in my industry call autodidacts, a fancy word to mean self-educated. As a programmer and data scientist, Brice commands exceptional technology talent—skills competitive with his college-educated peers. I suggest IL is not just a learning framework for people within formal learning structures, it benefits everyone.

Your IL success requires a self-evolution of personal learning processes and an internal desire to learn. By self-evolution, I mean your goals and dreams must have a committed connection to learning, the driving force for attaining and sustaining your personal and career growth and success. Understand that past learning challenges do not predict your future——I am a testament to this. Learning struggles are points in time; IL is the empowerment of becoming who you're meant to be.

I believe the future of IL will bring additional research to uncover new practical approaches to learning and development at all levels of educational institutions within the United States as it applies to the real-life context of learning experiences. We are merely at the starting point of future research examining expanded demographic characteristics of learners as applied to unstructured learning support for success. Are you ready for learning change? When you are, I hope you will embrace the strategies presented in this book as a tool of empowerment. Yes, it is unstructured, but it is powerful.

Summary

The future of learning will continue to become an important personal endeavor for life success. Each of us must learn to take control of our education. Whether we are talking about K-12, university, corporate or entrepreneurial purposes, attaining knowledge and skills will determine our future and success. The choices and methods of how we learn is a personal choice. I hope this book has provided you a model to effectively take control of your learning. Your success is the ability to bring the unstructured nature of informal learning outcomes to a place of self-empowerment.

APPENDIX A

Participant's Understanding of Informal Learning

Participant	Understanding of Informal Learning
Participant 1	"Someone takes it upon themselves to do naturally happens"
Participant 2	"Learn through experiment no structure"
Participant 3	"Usually, learner initiated they are kind of looking for it"
Participant 4	"Anything that is not specifically designed or structured by an organization or group"
Participant 5	"Learning that happens outside the classroom"
Participant 6	"Just reading on your own, on the job experience, research...structured by you and nobody else"
Participant 7	"What people do on their own outside of a structured environment"
Participant 8	"Learning that does not take place in a formal classroom"
Participant 9	"It's the additional material that I process outside of a given source"
Participant 10	"Learning without an educational institution learning from social media, learning from someone at work, learning from your peers outside of the school"

Unstructured

APPENDIX B

College-Level Examination

Course Area	Courses
Business	• Financial Accounting • Information Systems • Introductory Business Law • Principles of Management • Principles of Marketing
Composition & Literature	• American Literature • Analyzing and Interpreting Literature • College Composition • College Composition Modular • English Literature • Humanities
World Languages	• French Language: Levels 1 and 2 • German Language: Levels 1 and 2 • Spanish Language: Levels 1 and 2 • Spanish with Writing: Levels 1 and 2
History & Social Sciences	• American Government • History of the United States I: Early Colonization to 1877 • History of the United States II: 1865 to the Present • Human Growth and Development • Introduction to Educational Psychology • Introductory Psychology • Introductory Sociology • Principles of Macroeconomics • Principles of Microeconomics • Social Sciences and History

Course Area	Courses
	• Western Civilization I: Ancient Near East to 1648 • Western Civilization II: 1648 to the Present
Science & Mathematics	• Biology • Calculus • Chemistry • College Algebra • College Mathematics • Natural Sciences • Precalculus

FIGURES

TABLES

APPENDIX

ENDNOTES

Chapter 1

Barrett, J., & Brown, H. (2014). From learning comes meaning: Informal co-mentorship and the second-career academic in education. *The Qualitative Report, 19*(37), 1-15. Retrieved from https://nsuworks.nova.edu/tqr/vol19/iss37/1/

Campana, J. (2014). Learning for work and professional development: The significance of Informal Learning networks of digital media industry professionals. International Journal of Training Research, 12(3), 213-226. doi.org/10.1080/14480220.2014.11082043

Lee, W. O. (2014). Lifelong learning and learning to learn: An enabler of new voices for the new times. International Review of Education, 60(4), 463-479. doi.org/10.1007/s11159-014-9443-z

Lohman, M. C. (2009). A survey of factors influencing the engagement of information technology professionals in Informal Learning activities. Information Technology, Learning, and Performance Journal, 25(1), 43-53. Retrieved from https://www.learntechlib.org/j/ISSN-1535-1556/

Psychology Today (2021). Creativity. https://www.psychologytoday.com/us/basics/creativity. Psychology Today © 2021 Sussex Publishers, LLC

Watson, Richard A. "René Descartes." *Encyclopedia Britannica*, 27 Mar. 2021, https://www.britannica.com/biography/Rene-Descartes. Accessed 16 May 2021.

Chapter 2

Barrett, J., & Brown, H. (2014). From learning comes meaning: Informal co-mentorship and the second-career academic in education. *The Qualitative*

Report, 19(37), 1-15. Retrieved from
https://nsuworks.nova.edu/tqr/vol19/iss37/1/
Davison Munodawafa, Communication: concepts, practice and challenges, Health Education Research, Volume 23, Issue 3, June 2008, Pages 369–370, https://doi.org/10.1093/her/cyn024[2]
Mitic, I. (2021)/ Gig Economy Statistics: The New Normal in the Workplace. https://fortunly.com/statistics/gig-economy-statistics/#gref
Pierce, Rod. (29 Oct 2020). "About Math is Fun." Math Is Fun. Retrieved 14 Apr 2021 from
http://www.mathsisfun.com/aboutmathsisfun.html[2]
Psychology Today (2021). Creativity. https://www.psychologytoday.com/us/basics/creativity. Psychology Today © 2021 Sussex Publishers, LLC[1]

Chapter 3

Bandura, A. (1969). Social-learning theory of identificatory processes. In D. A. Goslin (Ed.), *Handbook of Socialization Theory and Research* (213-262). Skokie, IL: Rand McNally.
Carpenter-Aeby, T., & Aeby, V. G. (2013). Application of andragogy to instruction in an MSW practice class. *Journal of Instructional Psychology, 40*(1), 3-13. https://www.questia.com/library/p6137/journal-of-instructional-psychology
Chametzky, B. (2014). Andragogy and engagement in online learning: Tenets and solutions. *Creative Education, 5*(10), 813-821A. Doi.org/10.4236/ce.2014.510095[3]
Deeming, P., & Johnson, L. L. (2009). An application of Bandura's social learning theory: A new approach to deafblind support groups. *Journal of the American Deafness and Rehabilitation Association (JADARA),* 203-209. Retrieved from https://www.adara.org/[4]
Jamieson, P. (2009). The serious matter of informal learning. *Planning for Higher Education, 37*(2), 18-25. Retrieved from https://www.scup.org/page/phe?path=phe

Jonassen, D. H., & Rohrer-Murphy, L. (1999). Activity theory as a framework for designing constructivist learning environments. *Educational Technology, Research and Development, 47*(1), 61. doi.org/10.1007/BF02299477[6]

Hung, D., Tan, S., & Koh, T. (2006). From traditional to constructivist epistemologies: A proposed theoretical framework based on activity theory for learning communities. *Journal of Interactive Learning Research, 17*(1), 37-55. Retrieved from https://www.aace.org/pubs/jilr/[7]

Knowles, M. (1980). The modern practice of adult education (Vol. 41). New York, NY: Association Press.[1]

Lohman, M. C. (2009). A survey of factors influencing the engagement of information technology professionals in Informal Learning activities. *Information Technology, Learning, and Performance Journal, 25*(1), 43-53. Retrieved from *https://www.learntechlib.org/j/ISSN-1535-1556/*

Mintzes, J. J., Marcum, B., Messerschmidt-Yates, C., & Mark, A. (2013). Enhancing self-efficacy in elementary science teaching with professional learning communities. *Journal of Science Teacher Education, 24*(7), 1201-1218. doi.org/10.1007/s10972-012-9320-1

Pereira, R., Baranauskas, M. C. C., & da Silva, S. (2013). Social software and educational technology: Informal, formal and technical values. *Journal of Educational Technology & Society, 16*(1), 4-14. Retrieved from https://www.j-ets.net/ETS/index.html

Perry, R. B. (2009). Role modeling excellence in clinical nursing practice. *Nurse Education in Practice, 9*(1), 36-44. doi.org/10.1016/j.nepr.2008.05.001[5]

Puliyel, M. M., Puliyel, J. M., & Puliyel, U. (1999). Drawing on adult learning theory to teach personal and professional 5values. *Medical Teacher, 21*(5), 513-515. Doi.org/10.1080/01421599979211[2]

Taylor, M., King, J., Pinsent-Johnson, C., & Lothian, T. (2003). Collaborative practices in adult literacy programs. *Adult Basic Education, 13*(2), 81-99. Retrieved from http://epress.lib.uts.edu.au/journals/index.php/lnj/article/view/2207

Winters, F. I., and Alexander, P. A. Peer collaboration: The relation of regulatory behaviors to learning with hypermedia. *Instructional Science, 39*(4), 407-427. doi.org/10.1007/s11251-010-9134-5

Chapter 4

Combobox.com

My personal work/leisure/learning environment - The Ed Techie (typepad.co.uk)

Zoom Meetings - Zoom

Cynthia Vinney - What Is a Schema in Psychology? Definition and Examples (thoughtco.com)

Chapter 5

Johnson, D. W., & Johnson, R. (1975). Learning together and alone: Cooperation, competition, and individualization. Englewood Cliffs, NJ; Prentice-Hall.

Martinez, M. E. (2010). Learning and cognition: The design of the mind. Merrill. Upper Saddle River, New Jersey.

Reigeluth, C.M. and Carr-Chellman, A. A. (2002). Instructional-design theories and models: Building a common knowledge base (Volume III).

Chapter 6

The Center for Corporate and Professional Development (2021). Kent State University. https://www.kent.edu/yourtrainingpartner#

Chapter 7

Foorman BR, Schatschneider C, Eakin MN, Fletcher JM, Moats LC, Francis DJ. The impact of instructional practices in grades 1 and 2 on reading and spelling achievement in high poverty schools. Contemporary Educational Psychology. 2006;31:1–29. [Google Scholar]

Gabriel, M. A. (2004). Learning together: Exploring group interactions online. Journal of Distance Education, 19(1), 54-72. Retrieved from https://www.questia.com/library/p439531/journal-of-distance-education-online

Gray, B. (2004). Informal Learning in an online community of practice. Journal of Distance Education, 19(1), 20-35. Retrieved from https://www.questia.com/library/p439531/journal-of-distance-education-online[1]

Hung, D., Tan, S., & Koh, T. (2006). From traditional to constructivist epistemologies: A proposed theoretical framework based on activity theory for learning communities. Journal of Interactive Learning Research, 17(1), 37-55. Retrieved from https://www.aace.org/pubs/jilr/

Lebenicnik, M., Pitt, I., & Starcic, A. I. (2015). Use of online learning resources in the development of learning environments at the intersection of formal and informal learning: The student as autonomous designer. *CEPS Journal: Center for Educational Policy Studies Journal, 5*(2), 95-113. Retrieved from https://www.questia.com/library/p439417/ceps-journal-center-for-educational-policy-studies

Loombardi, P. (2013). Instructional methods, strategies and technologies to meet the needs of all learners. Press Books.

Chapter 8

Cunningham, J., & Hillier, E. (2013). Informal Learning in the workplace: Key activities and processes. Education & Training, 55(1), 37-51. Doi.org/10.1108/00400911311294960

Sangrà, A., & Wheeler, S. (2013). New informal ways of learning: Or are we formalizing the informal? Rusc, 10(1), 286-293. doi.org/10.7238/rusc.v10i1.1689Watkins, Bob. What does a DBA do all day? March 9 2006
https://www.techrepublic.com/article/just-what-does-a-dba-do-all-day/

Chapter 9

Barrett, J., & Brown, H. (2014). From learning comes meaning: Informal co-mentorship and the second-career academic in education. *The Qualitative Report, 19*(37), 1-15. Retrieved from
https://nsuworks.nova.edu/tqr/vol19/iss37/1/

Britannica, The Editors of Encyclopaedia. "Bill Gates". Encyclopedia Britannica, 17 May. 2021, https://www.britannica.com/biography/Bill-Gates.[1]

Hayashi, E. C. S., & Baranauskas, M. C. (2013). Affectability in educational technologies: A socio-technical perspective for design. *Journal of Educational Technology & Society, 16*(1), 57-n/a.[1]

Taylor, D. (2020). Does Bill Gates Have a College Degree?

Unstructured